THE

MAGIC SEVEN:

7 Steps to Perfect Spiritual Power

By

LIDA A. CHURCHILL

www.JonRosePublishing.com

Published by

JonRose
Publishing™

PMB 239
13 Summit Square Center
Langhorne, PA 19047-1098
800-582-4178
215-734-2288 fax
info@JonRosePublishing.com
www.JonRosePublishing.com

THE MAGIC SEVEN
by
Lida A. Churchill
Originally published in 1901

JonRose Publishing - Innovative eBooks
for your Health, Education and Enjoyment.

JonRose Publishing, JonRoseEBooks and logo are
registered trademarks of
JonRose Publishing, LLC

"I should have made it shorter if I had had time," was the reply of a noted clergyman when a listener complained that his sermon was too short.

The author of this book spent much time in making THE MAGIC SEVEN so short that it cannot only be carried in the pocket, but its contents be carried in the memory and the heart. It aims to eliminate all which would entangle the thought or confuse the mind, and to make plain a course by which mental powers may be utilized in all the affairs of life.

LIDA A. CHURCHILL

The

Magic Seven

Lida A. Churchill

The unseen forces are
the real forces.
By the persistent,
patient, intelligent
use of
the thought
implements,
you may put in
operation
power which is
Invincible.

TABLE OF CONTENTS

STEP ONE
HOW TO CENTER YOURSELF

What is meant by centering yourself? And why is such a process necessary?

"What," asked a young officer of an experienced general, "do you consider the first requisite for an army which is to be victorious?"

"That it be within always possible reach of an adequate base of supplies," was the reply.

In other words, no army can be sure of the brains which wisely plan, the strength which compels victory, the endurance which renders triumph permanent, without a center from which these things may be unfailingly called forth. An army may for a time subsist on forage, but such a subsistence can never be anything but precarious, and it is almost certain that the rations thus obtained will be insufficient and unsatisfactory, giving only spasmodic strength, and none of the confidence and mind-rest which come from a knowledge of sure available supplies.

The fact, then, becomes self-evident that an army's center is its base of supplies, without which it may be morally certain of disaster, if not of complete final defeat, and will degenerate into an ineffectual horde of marauders.

This is no truer of an army than of an individual. He must find his center around his base of supplies, and if he is to greatly achieve and finally win, these supplies must be suitable, adequate, and unfailing. One having no base of supplies may forage for a time, but such subsistence will leave him on the straggling, unwinning side.

Now, everyone has the natural and healthy wish to be on the winning side. The first thing, then, is to decide that for you, for everyone, no matter what his past or present, his heredity, age or environment, there is a winning side. If, from long habit of uncertainty and unfaith, one cannot thus decide, let him determine to find out whether it is true or not; and the way to do this is to *act exactly as though he believed it.*

"There's a brook just over the ridge," declared a man to two thirsty hunters. "I don't believe it," said one; "it's too rocky and barren about here for brooks." And he sat down. "I don't believe it, either," replied his companion, "but I'm going to see if it is true." He went, and came back with his flask full of water.

It being imperative that one who is to win must center in an always accessible and adequate base of supplies, it becomes necessary to determine where and of what nature this center shall be.

First, it must be where no one can bar him out from it, and, second, it must contain such stores as will give strength, confidence, and victory.

It is a truth attested by millions of cases that he who tries to form a base of supplies, make a center, outside of himself, and by things which are not inherently his, is likely at any hour, and almost certain in the end, to meet with the fate of the forager, which is moral vagabondage. One depending upon expectations from rich relatives, the influence of those in power, the chances of good luck, the power of beauty or diplomacy—anything which is not permanently and inherently his, which he cannot *command*, has no base of supplies, and is on the unwinning side.

Where and what is the center of one who is to win? It is *within his inmost self and those things which his thoughts, his desires, his practices, may make for him always available, must make for him actual working forces if he wills it so*.

"We are thirsty, give us water," called the captain of a craft to the commander of another craft. "Let down your buckets," came back the answer; "you are at the mouth of the Amazon."

You who have not begun your base of supplies, do not even realize that you may have one, who are foraging, and consequently thirsting, despairing, failing, are at the mouth of the Amazon, and by flinging out your bucket may dip up all that will make you successful. The recognition that you, individualized so sharply that you are unlike any other person in the world, are still a part of the great universal Force and Intelligence, as the unduplicated wave is a part of the sea, and that of these things which saturate you and flow around you, you may use as much as you will to any purpose you wisely and deliberately choose, this recognition must be your bucket, and Will must send it out and draw it, filled, home to you.

You have, then, must have if you are certainly to win, as your base of supplies, *all that God is or owns.* How shall you use what is thus made possible to you so as to render it a never-failing working force?

You must *learn* to use it by taking certain exercises intelligently, persistently, unfailingly. No other methods will suffice.

Thousands who have given years to the study of music, languages, or other accomplishments, are impatient if they cannot learn how to become spiritually strong and effectual in a day or a week. They want the most precious possessions, those that will make them free, happy, opulent, without paying for them in time, attention, or persistence. Know, once for all, that for the diamond of spiritual effectiveness you must delve with no easy or intermittent thrusts, but be comforted by the truth that he who digs for it does so by no severer labor, no more persistent endeavor and attention than are put forth by one who seeks a common stone, and, in the end, he holds as his own *nothing less than a diamond.*

SUMMARY AND EXERCISE:

You must, to be successful, center in an always accessible, permanent, and adequate base of supplies. This base of supplies is yours at your insistent and persistent demand, and with it you may do what you intelligently decide to do, become what you intelligently decide to become.

Say every day, in the silence of your heart, reverently, earnestly, repeating the words till they *sink into your consciousness:*

I am depending upon nothing but God. I am a part of the All-Wisdom, the All-Intelligence, the All-Strength, the All-Power, the All-Peace, the All-Opulence, and I am able to utilize all these Forces.

STEP TWO
HOW TO GO INTO THE SILENCE

How shall you gain and keep the poise necessary to the absorption and utilization of the powers which insure victory?

Engrave it on your heart and burn it into your memory that, as Emerson declares, "All power is in silent moments." Every great deed was accomplished in the silence of some brain and heart before the instruments which made the world aware of the victory came into action. As the flame is not the real fire, but the sign and outcome of the fire, so accomplishment is not the real force, but the sign and outcome of the force. The real crucifixion was in Gethsemane. Waterloo was won in Wellington's tent.

The Angelus was painted in Millet's brain. All great causes in all the worlds are ever silent, and ever silently conceived.

Water which swirls and foams admits of no reflection. Everyone who has had his picture taken can recall the photographer's request, "Now remain perfectly quiet."

Why was this quiet necessary? Because the sensitized plate would otherwise produce nothing but an incoherent unlikeness to anything which the sitter desired. The mind is a sensitized plate, and he who is to receive the impression which will result in the most satisfactory action must have his mind quiet. "Be still, and know that I am God." Still, because in no other way can you come into intelligent and vital touch with the All-Love, All-Power, All-Opulence.

You have, at some time, doubtless, tried to give counsel, direction, or encouragement to an extremely excited, hurried, or worried person. You probably did not succeed to any satisfactory degree. Why? Because—and here is a second truth to engrave upon the heart and burn in upon the memory—*two are required in the giving of a gift, the receiving of a message. God Himself cannot give you anything which you are unwilling or unready to receive.*

A lady asked a friend to bring her a certain remedy of which the latter had spoken, and the next evening was named as the time when the remedy should be brought. When the friend appeared to keep the appointment, the lady, forgetting that such an appointment had been made, had locked her door and gone to the next room to call. The friend went away. "Why," said the lady afterward, "did you not just bang my door, and demand entrance? I should probably have heard you if you had made enough noise?"

The Great Commissary who has charge of your supplies is willing to send to your door all that you can need or intelligently desire, but you will never, can never, receive these supplies unless you are willing and ready to receive them. He does not bang at doors or demand entrance. "Wilt thou be made whole?" was the question of the Christ to one who needed healing. The power which could raise the dead and still the turmoil of Nature never disregarded man's free will. "Behold, I stand at the door and knock," said this same great Master. "If any man will hear my voice, and open the door, I will come in and sup with him."

Mark you, He stands and knocks, but if you would receive Him and all that He brings, you, yourself, must *open the door*. Never dream that God reveals himself or gives His gifts *whether or no!*

Another very important step toward creating a receptive soul-center is the pruning process, cutting off habits or things which excite, depress, or discourage you. The intoxicated or unduly excited or depressed brain, whether these things come from drink, drugs or unwise companionship, very seriously hinder or wholly forbid the poise which makes for power, peace, and opulence. The tongue must be taught silence. All quarrels and argument must be strictly tabooed. In wrangling or arguing one mind is clashing against another, which causes a shock to both, and all shocks are destructive of receptivity, and in many cases prevent for many days together a return to the heart silence which is alone effective of good results. For it is a heart silence to which we must attain. Most of us must live for many hours each day in the midst of outside noises, and long stillnesses of the hands are, to the majority, impossible. But, like those places fathoms deep in the sea which no storms reach, no turmoil disturbs, so the inner chamber of one's being may be still whatever the outward conditions. And, mark you, all disturbing influences must be pruned away. One breeze which tosses its surface into foam, or an upheaval of mud from its bottom, will as effectively destroy the power of the lake to reflect as would storm and wind and mud upheaval all together.

"Why," exclaims one, "this means a wholly new mode of life!"

Verily, it means no less.

And right here is a place to do some serious thinking, to come to a momentous decision. Have the intoxications, the quarrellings, the arguments, the excitements by people or things, brought you any substantial good, any permanent happiness, any power, peace or opulence? If not, is it not the part of wisdom to cut them off, that in their stead may sprout and grow those things which can but mean permanent betterment? If you cannot, from experience, observation, or imagination, decide that you have enough of them, that you will leave your delving for the common stone of mere stimulation and dig for the diamond of real happiness, you are not ready to receive this diamond.

Take what you are ready for, what you really want, and *pay for it*. This is the mandate of the law. Work with the law and have all things. Work against or disregard the law, and have nothing worth having, nothing which will remain. All things are yours, but you must claim them aright. Go into the silent center of your being, and learn of God.

SUMMARY AND EXERCISE:

All power is generated, all great things conceived, in the stillness of the soul-center, which one may learn to keep always undisturbed, and hence at all times capable of receiving impressions from the All-Intelligence, All-Power. One must be ready to receive, or nothing is given him. Every influence which disturbs the receptivity of the mind must be cut off. A new mode of life must be adopted and fostered.

Say every day, in the quiet of your room, or elsewhere:

I am still of heart and of tongue. I invite, and hold myself in the attitude to receive, the Intelligence which teaches, the Love which protects and satisfies, the Power which makes invincible, the Peace which blesses. I admit nothing into my life which would prevent or hinder the greatest soul receptivity. I wait in the Silence with and for God.

STEP THREE
HOW TO CONCENTRATE
THE MIND

How shall you bring the wisdom and force which you gain in the centered life and silenced soul into effective action?

"Will a pound of feathers come to the ground with as much force as a pound of lead?" asked a teacher of the child, Gail Hamilton. "Yes, if you roll 'em *just as tight*," replied the future author.

What gives a piece of dynamite which you could easily hold in your hand, power to demolish a huge building or rend a solid rock? Focalized force, or concentration. A certain river flowed into numerous small outlets, wandered away into tiny side-streams, and so meandered, with its diminished volume and ineffectual flow, to its mouth. One day this river was dammed above the wasteful side-streams, and by confinement to one place grew into a mighty force. When it burst away from its trammels, and sent its gathered might against a populous town, that town was swept before its strength like a straw before a cyclone. It was concentration which destroyed Johnstown.

The train moves, the car is propelled, because the steam or the electricity is gathered at one point for one purpose. There might be just as much diffused steam or electricity trying to move half a dozen different things, and little or nothing would be accomplished. The difference between diffused and focalized steam or electricity is the difference between the pound of loose feathers and the pound of lead.

Before an army can be sent out to sure victory, its ranks must be gathered at one place. So before your thought forces can win for you the things you desire, they must be brought home, focalized, concentrated.

What is concentration?

"Carlyle deafened the world to insure silence," declares Professor Wilkinson. Many people are so determined to concentrate that they render concentration impossible. They sit bolt upright, stiff and rigid, clutch the arms of their chairs, shut their lips tightly, and command their minds to become fixed on some point, phrase, or word—thus putting the thing they demand out of the question. It requires all their attention to preserve this fixed and rigid attitude.

Now, concentration is not a mental clutching of something, a spasmodic projection of the mind toward something, or an anxious demand for something. The greatest mental as well as physical power—for there is a great deal of mental noise—is silent, and has the appearance of negation. The thunder roars and hurtles, but does no execution; the lightning, with never a sound, withers and destroys, or, under control, propels our railroad trains and street cars, bearing forward tons of weight. The mountain brook tumbles and froths and bubbles, and may be heard a long distance away; the Mississippi, with sufficient volume to float thousands of people and tons of merchandise, is serene, and utterly silent in its flow. A flock of wild geese will make more noise than the emptying of the St. Lawrence into the Gulf. Concentration, which is conceded by all to be one of the greatest forces of the world, is as noiseless as the lightning, as calm as the flow of the Mississippi. It is like a ray of the sun which goes swiftly, silently, un-spasmodically to the heart of the thing whereunto it is sent, and closes around and grapples it as the sun closes around and grapples the moisture which it lifts from lake to cloud. It is gathering all one's mental force to a single point for the single purpose of sending it, fully freighted, to the heart of the matter with which one is concerned.

Concentration, in a word, means controlling one's thoughts instead of allowing one's thought to control him. That this can be done, the author has conclusively and repeatedly proved by various experiments, one of which is to write, or to sit without occupation, for an hour at a time surrounded by scores of talking people without allowing one intelligible word of the conversation to reach her consciousness, or else by ceasing to think at all. Perfection in concentration, like perfection in anything else, must come by faithful, continued practice. Spasmodic efforts will do little or no good; but the faithful student, by the constant practice outlined below, will soon be enabled to call his wandering thoughts home, to shut out any disagreeable or disturbing sound or sensation, and to focus the mind at any time, on any subject, with the result of doing what was formerly, perhaps, an hour's mental work, such as studying, composing, creating plots or plans, in twenty minutes. It will also enable him to make of his thoughts one thought which will prove a dynamic power to change all things for him.

Do not be discouraged if for a long time during your concentration hour foreign thoughts keep intruding. This is the common experience of all. *Keep going back to your center*, and after a little while you will be surprised and gratified to realize, even though you are able to fix your absolute attention on any point for only two or three minutes without the interruption of other thoughts, how rapidly and surely you have gained in mental power.

Do not strive, fret or be discouraged, but keep up religiously the daily practice, and be sure of ultimate victory.

Under no circumstances should one who would attain to perfect concentration wear at any time uncomfortable clothing or shoes. The disagreeable sensations caused by these things will, unless you are very advanced, claim much of your thought.

SUMMARY AND EXERCISE:

All force, to be effective, must be brought to a point, concentrated. All force thus concentrated is a mighty power. This power is still, and has the appearance of negation. Concentration may be cultivated until it becomes invincible.

Take some part of every day or evening when you are sure you will not be interrupted. Let every article of clothing for the body and feet, and your position, be entirely comfortable, that no consciousness of discomfort may distract your attention.

Having put yourself entirely at ease, rest your head on the back of the chair, or let it droop forward, and look in imagination *within yourself* at a point directly back of the pit of the stomach, where lies the solar plexus, which occultists call "the king brain." Imagine there a point of yellow light. Sit *perfectly still*, fixing, as nearly as possible, the *whole attention* on this point of light, **thinking of nothing else**. Continue this from twenty to forty minutes. You will find this very difficult at first, but every day it will come easier, and before very long you will be able to hold your entire attention for a number of minutes at a time at *one single point*.

After thus practicing for a short time, in many cases in a week or two, you may, during your concentration hour, put a word—such as "will," "love," "life," etc.—or a phrase, or the image of a friend in place of the point of light, and keep your mind fixed on this word, phrase, or friend.

Step Four
How To Command Opulence

Of what avail shall be your massed thought force? The great test question concerning anything is, Is it of use? The water of the river may as well have wandered away in wasteful streams, the steam have escaped in thin and separate jets, the electricity have spread itself through hundreds of feet of air, if the focused water, steam, or electricity could not be and was not utilized to a desired end. If you cannot accomplish something, gain some object, by your gathered thought, then the time and effort used in the gathering have been wasted.

This brings us to another fact which, if you are to obtain and utilize your possible power, must be written on the heart and burnt into the memory. In using occult means you are not dealing with vague, misty, uncertain forces, but with the *most powerful and certain agents which can possibly be employed.* Occult means hidden. The forces you employ are hidden from sight, touch, sound, or smell. There is no truer declaration than that "spiritual things must be spiritually discerned."

"Give us something tangible," cries the so-called realist, "something which chemistry can analyze, science can demonstrate." Now it is, to anyone who will give the subject five minutes' intelligent thought, a proved statement that not one of the most real and effectual forces of the world can be analyzed by chemistry or demonstrated by science. What is the passion which has wrought most mightily for the world's blessedness, which has populated it, created its homes, generated its courage, nursed its noble- ness, developed its unselfishness, inspired its orators, authors, painters, poets, saints, kept its heart warm, given it splendidly effective life? Love.

What passion has ever devastated, tortured, and ruined? Hate.

What feeling, no matter what the discouragement of circumstances or the denials of environment, keeps thousands of the world's workers toiling at their tasks? Enthusiasm.

What sends men to die for their country, or prompts them to forego all that their natures crave, that the demands of justice may be met? Honor.

What draws thousands to hear a man's speech, or to touch his hand, and makes him like a god in power? Magnetism.

Can the chemist analyze, or the scientist tabulate, the properties of love, hate, enthusiasm, honor, or magnetism?

Who can weigh, measure, or explain the sensa- tions of joy, grief, attraction or repulsion? Which of the world's greatest scientists has not stood dumb before the question, What is Life?

And it has been proved beyond a doubt that the occult forces, of which we have named a few, are intelligent, effective powers, the very best implements for building up and securing an opulent life; for opulence, which surely means money, means, as surely, everything else which the heart can desire.

At Ashley-Downs, England, George Muller established, without a word of solicitation, one act of worldly manipulation, the Orphan-House which has grown to such huge proportions. In Boston, Dr. Charles Cullis raised and supported, wholly without visible means, his Consumptives' and Orphans' Homes. Both depended solely upon the faith which *holds*, the prayer which *refuses denial*. The beautiful town of Seabreeze, Florida, was built by Helen Wilmans' mental demands.

The writer has in mind several individuals personally known to her, who in the space of three or four years have, by the use of thought forces, lifted themselves from adverse and discouraging conditions to pleasant and profitable ones, which are continually improving.

Why do so few improve their lot by the use of these forces? Because so few accept them as forces, or put them into operation.

Having decided that our mental implements are real and effective forces, what then? Bring them to bear upon your case. How?

"I think," said a man in a restaurant, "that I'll have chicken, or perhaps steak would be better; or maybe oysters would suit me best of all. I don't know just what I want, or can pay for."

"I cannot serve you till you decide," replied the waiter.

Now, the first thing in trying to better your condition is to *know what you want*, and what you can, in money, talent or experience, *pay for*. Nothing and nobody can serve you till you decide these questions. If it is success in an occupation on which you wish to concentrate, first decide what occupation you will choose. The theory that one may be anything he desires to be is sheer nonsense unless he desires to be something for which he has an inherent capability or talent. Many people wish to do certain things merely because these things are considered superior to ordinary occupations, without regard to their own fitness to take them up. I have in mind one who strongly desires to be a great writer, and another who as strongly desires to be a great public singer. The one cannot write even an intelligent letter, the other cannot fill acceptably even a drawing-room engagement. Neither can pay the price in the only acceptable coin, which is fitness, for the desired success, and life-long concentration would never make either proficient in the chosen occupation. "The soul's emphasis is always right," says Emerson. Neither of these people has chosen according to the soul's emphasis, which is the emphasis of sense and potential capability.

But *decide the question yourself.* Every year the lives and careers of thousands are mutilated or ruined because those thousands yield to the opinions of others rather than respect and obey their own convictions.

Having sensibly decided what you want, you wish to bring all visible and invisible aid and influence to bear upon it. You, perhaps, wish to better a business already established; to bring harmony out of disharmony; to make an unpaying business pay; to create a reconciliation; to receive wisdom or direction upon some subject. No matter what you wish, proceed in the same way.

Never allow yourself to worry or to be despondent about the thing you have undertaken. Realize that you have put your demand into the thought realm, the most powerful of all realms, and feel as confident and easy as though you had placed it in the hands of a trusted agent. Know that mental laws, rightly used, insure perfect results.

Do not talk unnecessarily about your business. Much talk is disbursive of strength and cohesion. Especially, never speak of it to an unsympathetic person who would create about you an atmosphere of doubt or unbelief. Always think of yourself as *already possessing* the thing you desire.

Be patient. A feeling of hurry and impatience impedes matters. Calmness will be one of your most powerful allies. Things are done by effect following cause, and the law must have time for its effective working. Often things become apparently worse before they grow better. This is usually the upheaval of old conditions before the advent of the new. Bear it as bravely as possible, *constantly expecting the dawn of the new day.*

When you see the opportunity for action, *act promptly and fearlessly,* and according to your own judgment.

This concentration hour must be *rigidly* and *continuously* observed. Spasmodic and intermittent efforts and attention will never bring satisfactory results. Vigilance here, as elsewhere, is the price of success.

These instructions, like all others in this book, apply to people of all ages and in all conditions of life.

SUMMARY AND EXERCISE:

Unused and unusable things are valueless. Your massed thoughts, in order to benefit you, must be sent out to accomplish the thing you desire. The unseen forces are the real forces. By the persistent, patient, intelligent use of the thought implements you may put in operation power which is invincible.

Go *every day* where you can be alone for at least twenty minutes; an hour is far better. Loosen every article of clothing, and sit perfectly at ease.

Take all the tension off yourself. Let go of every clutching, depressing, impatient thought. Focus your mind calmly, unspasmodically, but unwaveringly and forcefully, upon the matter in mind. State your will concerning it as lucidly and with as much assurance as you would state your orders for goods to a merchant, and try to feel as much assurance of being adequately served as you would in speaking to the merchant.

Then *listen*, and *expect answers*. After a time, if you practice faithfully, you will receive these answers in the shape of suggestions, new thoughts and fresh ideas; the assurance you will probably at first be obliged to assume, will become real, and you will find new opportunities coming to you, will meet the people who can serve you, and will find your way out of your difficulties as the sun breaks through the morning mist.

STEP FIVE
HOW TO USE THE WILL

How shall you hold your new resolves, your freshly generated thoughts and practices in place and to their work until they become as much a part of your daily life as breath itself? This they must become to prove effective or adequate.

Why does a cattle-raiser brand the mark upon his stock? Why are important documents signed in ink? Have you ever seen a printer's "form"? When every piece of type is in place, the words and sentences are held securely together by a "chase," a solid iron rim, until the collected mass has been used to indelibly stamp the desired page. Occasionally the "chase" slips, letting the type separate, thus somewhat damaging the page, or allowing the letters to fall into a confused mass which means nothing, spells nothing, and is of no use until the type is assorted and again set up, a process much more bewildering and difficult than the first arrangement of the form.

Your thoughts must be branded in, held in place, until they spell out your life-page in bold, comprehensive, indelible sentences. If they slip and become confused, your life-page must be marred. If they fall into an incoherent mass, they cannot, unless gathered up and rearranged—and the rearrangement of once adjusted thoughts and purposes is far harder and more bewildering than the first adjustment—be of the least benefit.

Will must be the "chase" which keeps your thoughts, which are your forces, in place, until they do their required work. It must also be the flaming sword to guard you from those things which are foreign to and destructive of the high, effective life. What is the Will? Let us first see what it is not. It is not something which brawls and vociferates, which clinches the fist, reddens the face, and embitters the speech. These things denote the absence of will, of which, self-control is one of the chief attributes. We sometimes say of a person that he "flies all to pieces." This, so far as all the real part of him is concerned, is literally true. He scatters all his force, thus becoming impotent and ineffective for aught but evil. You may say you have seen or heard of many forceful deeds which were done under the impetus of anger. So has everyone, but the force thus exerted was almost never productive of good.

Murders, quarrels, antagonisms, with all their attendant heartbreak, demoralization and loss, are the results of this force. Insanity—with the exception of the extremely rare cases where it is justifiable and righteous, anger is insanity—engenders and is met by insanity, and the results are present chaos and havoc and future loss and unhappiness. Think not for a moment that because you are often angry, or allow your anger to have vent in word or deed, that you have a strong will. Know, rather, that your will- power is weak, and that there is great need of strengthening it.

Again, blind, unreasoning stubbornness is not will. Will is intelligent, and capable, when necessity demands, of flexibility. Stubbornness is stupid and rigid.

Perhaps you were reared in a place where wood was used for fuel. If so, you have probably been where the attempt was made to cook, and to heat the room, by hemlock sticks, which crackle and snap and blaze up furiously, sooting many things, burning food on one side and leaving it half raw on the other, throwing out for a little time a burning, untempered heat, and then sinking into dead blackness. You probably have afterward witnessed the silent, steady glow of a deep coal fire, noted how perfectly it did its work of cooking and heating, and how hour after hour its force remained the same. These two fires illustrate the difference between the riot of passion, the black inefficiency of stubbornness, and the still, efficient, lasting fire of coal.

A life ungoverned by a developed will may be like the meteor, brilliant and interesting for a time, but, like the meteor, its course will be erratic, and its usual tendency downward; while the will-governed life is kept in its orbit among the grand spaces, along a purposeful, upward way.

Man's will is his individualized God-power, and when conjoined to the great ocean of force and intelligence in which he, consciously or unconsciously, has his being, his word becomes God's word, his concentrated and projected thought the very power of God in operation.

God's word, I say. But, mark you, the word must be spoken as God would speak it, meant as God would mean it, with every fiber of the soul, the brain, the body. The word which holds, accomplishes, revolutionizes, which cannot return void, is the decree which goes forth from the inmost chamber of man's being.

Someone may say he has a weak will, or almost no will at all, and, therefore, cannot expect it to accomplish much. What then? How does a child learn to walk steadily? By walking, and continuing to walk. How does an author learn to write strongly, an artist to paint effectively? By never ceasing, through long years, to paint and write. One must learn to will adequately by constantly willing, and, as the child, the author, the artist grows stronger and surer in methods and results with every effort, so will it be with one's willing.

Among the first things with which the soul which is to win has to do are the will-nots. He must decide that he will not allow any habit which clogs his mentality and retards his spiritual growth; that he will not consort with those who are antagonistic to or unsympathetic with his ideas; that he will not admit aught which hampers or hinders his upward course. These will-nots must prove the knife which prunes away from his life-tree the entangling weeds, suffocating twigs, and poisonous parasites which would stunt its growth, render less strong its unfolding, or less wholesome and life-promoting its sap.

Then comes the positive, creative wills. Know for a certainty that nothing grows more rapidly or sturdily than, by constant use, the will. Many a soul who a few months ago was suffering, despairing, because it could not speak the creative word, is today rejoicing in its overcoming and accomplishment because it began using the will it had, and found the increase and consequent gain so quick, sure, and abundant.

One point never to be lost sight of is that in willing, as in most things, "now is the day of salvation." Never say that just this time you will take the stimulant, just this time seek the harmful acquaintance or place, just this time allow your usually silent hour to be used for some other purpose. Every time this occurs your will is weakened, your hour of victory postponed. Remember that "Will is destiny," and that whenever you strengthen your will you improve your destiny.

SUMMARY AND EXERCISE:

Will holds your thoughts in place and to their work. Neither anger nor stubbornness is will. Will is quiet, steady, intense, and, when developed and conjoined to the All-Will, invincible. It may be rapidly strengthened by constant use. It shapes destiny.

Say in the silence: *I will not to indulge in anything which hampers, or to associate with anyone who hinders my spiritual growth.* (Specific things or names may be used when desirable.) *I will not to be angry, or stubborn, or unduly elated or depressed concerning anything. I will not to be sick, or poor, or less than I am capable of being or becoming. I will to have a free, grand, effective manhood or womanhood. I will to be whatever I intelligently desire to be. I will to know God, to speak His Word, and to obtain His results.*

STEP SIX
HOW TO INSURE
PERFECT HEALTH

How shall you be able at all times, to sustain the vigorous thought, keep at full pressure the will by which your word becomes God's word?

Last winter those New Yorkers who used gas for cooking and lighting purposes were one day obliged to go to bakeries or restaurants for food, and to utilize their oil lamps for illuminating purposes. Nothing could be had from the gas jets except pale, feeble, intermittent flickers with no power, or warmth, or warrant of continuance. Extreme cold had frozen and demoralized the pipes. The gas was at the source of supply, ready to be made use of, but it had no fitting conductor through which it could flow to the place where its services were needed.

The great supply of force, heat, light, comfort is always ready at the source, but thousands of bodies make for it such poor conductors that only feeble and spasmodic flickers of it are seen.

What was done to those demoralized pipes that they might again become equal to the demands upon them?

First, there was a determination that the pipes should be repaired, and the work to that end was immediately begun. What if those in charge of the matter had decided that the gas consumers could get along with that pale, flickering, spasmodic flame, that they could help out with oil or coal stoves, and suffer from any consequent inconvenience? The result would have been deprivation, negation, and wholly unnecessary loss.

Secondly, there was a change of temperature, which released the pipes from unnatural rigidity and unequal pressure. Then, the joints where the small pipes had been torn away from the main pipe were remade, and the rents and ravages caused by abnormal conditions were repaired.

In other words, these nearly negative pipes—for there is some degree of life in everything—were put under the control of man's positive thought, and the conductor and thing to be conducted came into right relations.

In the beginning is the Word, always. He who is to have perfect health must determine that no pale, flickering, spasmodic life, which must be helped out by drugs or by any outside means whatever, will do for him; that he will have perfect health.

Secondly, he must avoid an atmosphere which would place or keep him in a rigid condition, or put him under unequal moral, mental, or spiritual pressure. Perfect health means perfect equilibrium of all one's being, and he who overlooks the matter of mental atmosphere overlooks one of the most vital factors in insuring or destroying health. One should never have for house-mate or frequent associate a person— and each of you knows at least one such— who renders spontaneity, free flow of thought and speech, or a peaceful state of mind impossible. It is no more healthy for him to be closely or frequently associated with such a person than it would be for a sensitive plant to be put to grow beside an iceberg, which would congeal its sap and render abortive the warmth of the sun, or beside a blazing fire which would scorch or wither it.

Where close association with a health-destroying person cannot, without disloyalty, dishonor, or self-ishness be avoided, it should be borne without anger or argument, and with as little mental disquietude as possible. Above all, there should be a fixed, persistent demand for a harmonious readjustment of life and its affairs.

Silence of tongue and heart is here, as elsewhere, the great bulwark against demoralization.

Again, companions or associates should never be chosen or retained because some other person finds them good or helpful. Carbonic acid gas, which is the very breath of vegetable life, is death or detriment to human beings. So one who is like the breath of life to another may be poison to you. He is both just and wise who chooses for companions and associates those with whom his higher nature blends as in the rainbow each hue blends with its corresponding color.

It may be urged that the fully spiritualized soul can bear anything undisturbed. True! But the great majority of souls are not fully spiritualized, and their progress toward this state is impeded by inharmonious influences, and there is a vast difference between endurance even of things by which one is not disturbed, and the full, buoyant vitality giving happiness without which no spiritualized soul has received, in full measure, its own. The greatest cause of the severance of one's individual pipe from the great main Pipe of health, is fear; and nothing does more to engender and keep alive fear than learning the names and dwelling upon the symptoms of diseases, as set forth by medical publications or unwisely learned individuals.

This dwelling upon names and symptoms gives suggestions upon which even the most normal mind is almost sure to act in a greater or less degree. Many of you will recall Jerome K. Jerome's hero, who, after a prolonged study of a medical work, declared that he had had "everything spoken of in the book except housemaid's knee," and wondered why this complaint had slighted him. A certain physician recently declared that when he was studying medicine he actually suffered to some extent from each disease about which he read. Another doctor deplored the fact that his wife had such free and constant access to his medical works, as by their perusal she was continually imagining that every slight ailment meant some of the dire complaints of which she had been reading, and, though naturally one of the healthiest of women, was, by fear and imagination, kept almost constantly ill.

Mary A. Livermore, speaking of a time, many years ago, when the plague visited Chicago, and she for several weeks went freely—and diseaseless—among the worst cases, determined, if possible, to learn what this dread disease was, and what its preventive and cure, declared that for one person who died of the plague a hundred died from fear of it or the belief that they had it.

Sudden deaths have many times multiplied since such terrifying names as cerebro-spinal meningitis, appendicitis, peritonitis, and others of half-understood import, have been added to the medical vocabulary. Often from insignificant attacks of pain, fear conjures up one of these dreaded ailments, and, in numerous cases, patients die—from names.

Why is it that for the past few years influenza has every winter become epidemic? There seems to be no better reason than that in these modern times influenza, which is simply a bad cold, has been rebaptized as La Grippe, and the term conveys to the popular imagination something far more dangerous and lasting than the word influenza, or cold. About the only thing that is clearly and generally understood about

La Grippe is that its first symptom is a cold, and so most people have come to fancy as soon as they take cold that they have, or shall have, La Grippe, and fear and imagination make, in thousands of cases, a severe, perhaps a fatal, illness.

It may be said that physicians and nurses are continually reading or thinking about or meeting disease, but are still among the healthiest people living. This proves, rather than disproves, our theory. They have, as a class, cast fear of names, disease, hardship, everything out of their minds, and this, with cleanliness, proper habits, and nourishing diet, immunizes their lives from harm.

Dwelling upon and rehearsing one's own symptoms or ailments is still more detrimental than reading about those of others, or symptoms or diseases in the abstract. The nearer a suggestion comes home, the greater hypnotizing power it has.

Once more, the body which is to be perfectly whole, must be clean. Remember that there is an overflow as well as an inflow of divine vitality. Much of the breath of life comes by absorption through the pores of the skin, as the spiritual breath comes of absorption by the spiritual pores. The clogging of the physical, as of the spiritual, pipes, by material or mental filth renders the free access and transmission of vitality quite impossible.

"Has your *protégé* come into the Kingdom of Heaven?" asked an evangelist of a man who had taken a most disreputable looking and tattered tramp as a helper, with a view to the latter's redemption.

"No," was the reply, "but he's in the place which is a sort of vestibule to the Kingdom of Heaven."

"What is that?" was the next inquiry.

"The Kingdom of Soap Suds," replied the reformer. "There's a kind of sympathetic chord running between cleanliness and godliness, and when a man begins to systematically wash his face and then his person, I know I may bring on my spiritual ethics with a hope of winning."

The truth is, everything which makes one feel more like a man teaches him more of the feeling of a god, and since almost everyone who conceives an intelligent idea of good things conceives, also, a desire for those things, and, as desire rules action, a feeling of respectability is one of the first forerunners of everything man can wish.

To this end, that one may step from commonplace manhood to invincible godhood, he should dress and live in a manner which will never detract from his idea of thorough respectability and ease of mind. And that he may so live, he should secure for himself a position by which self-respect, self-confidence, and the development of his best faculties are encouraged and sustained, and an income commensurate to his reasonable demands is assured.

Success which leaves the heart pure, the head clear, the moral growth un-retarded, is one of the greatest health-promoters and preservers. While wealth slays its thousands, and can be, and so often is, made a curse, poverty, with its train of degradation, soul and body starvation, arrest of development, and spirituality-murder, slays its tens of thousands.

He who is to be perfectly healthy must learn to fill his physical being with the breath which reaches and purifies and strengthens every part of it. In the exercise, at the close of this chapter, directions for using such breath are given.

Let no one dream that he or she can become healthy by pouring down drugs. Millions are every year trying this method and failing of their object. "Why don't you take your medicine?" recently asked a physician's wife of her husband, who was ill, and for whom another physician had prescribed "I know its worthlessness too well," was the reply. Everywhere honest physicians are admitting that drugs are, in a large majority of cases, merely suggestions, and are used oftener experimentally than scientifically.

Sunshine, exercise and air are a trio which must be made the constant companion of one who is to have perfect health. Nothing in the world, least of all man, grows and develops, and waxes from strength to strength, in the absence of light, heat and movement.

Cheerfulness, hope and faith are a second trio which makes tremendously for vitality.

Underlying, closing about, capping your vitality arch must be the Will, which shuts out devastation, shuts in power and strength, and makes you the creator and preserver of perfect health.

SUMMARY AND EXERCISE:

The great supply of health and strength is always ready, but many are not in a condition to receive it. The first step toward securing this condition is a determination to have it. Inharmonious people, uncleanliness, fear, uncongenial surroundings, unfit clothing, a position which does not foster self- respect and insure development, an inadequate income, and drugs, are detrimental to health. Sunshine, air, exercise, faith, and cheerfulness are great health preservers and promoters.

Say in the silence: *I will to have perfect health. I will to be in constant connection with the great Health Source. I will to have only such companions, thoughts, surroundings, practices, as will give me the God vitality, power, and peace.*

Sit upright. Place your hands on your knees, the fingers slightly over the edge of the knee-pan. Draw in a full, long breath, *which you can hear,* letting the abdomen expand to its full limit. Hold the breath as long as possible. While drawing in and holding, keep the idea that you are taking in Life, Strength, Vitality, using any of these words which you choose. When letting out the breath, so you *can hear it*, hold the idea that your weakness is going out with it. See that with the outgoing breath the abdomen is drawn completely in.

This exercise will assist you materially in concentrating the mind, and in inducing sleep.

STEP SEVEN
HOW TO ASK AND RECEIVE

How shall you demand in a way which cannot be denied? Did Jesus mean anything, in a literal, practical sense, when he said that if one asked aright he might have whatsoever he asked? One great mission of the so-called New Thought — which is, really, as old as the first thought of God — is to make plain the fact that Jesus meant, in a practical, everyday sense, everything which He, in giving counsel or enforcing lessons, said.

There, must be, if the word of Jesus be true, a way of asking which precludes any possibility of refusal. That there is such a way thousands, many of whom have been, hitherto, weak and impotent—or thought themselves so—are, thanks to the New-Old Thought, constantly proving.

What gives a request the character and power of a demand that must be met? First, the possession of something. A man walks into a bank, presents a piece of paper, and receives in money the amount specified on the check. No denial is possible. He has in that bank a sum of money, and no one can refuse his appropriation of it. Had he no funds there, he might present a thousand checks, and ask ever so earnestly to have one of them cashed, but he would receive nothing. Possibly some bystander might, from pity or some other cause, give or lend him a sum of money, but that would be very uncertain.

Having nothing to draw from, his request would not be a command, and would have no power. He could not ask aright.

A soldier is requested by his general to execute a commission, and the thing is unhesitatingly done. The possession of authority makes the general's request a command. A thousand other men might request the doing of the same deed, and remain unheeded. Having no power, they could not ask aright.

We say, and truly, that the skilled architect, engineer, or mechanic "commands" high wages. One of these asks for a responsible and high salaried position, and receives it, because he possesses that which renders his request a command.

A man might pray a hundred days, from his very soul, and with fasting, that he might draw money from a bank, might be served by a subordinate, might be placed in a responsible position with a high salary, but unless he possessed the money, the authority, the skill, his prayers would be, for the time being at least, futile.

Prayer has come largely to be looked upon in one of two ways, as a useless, superstitious formula, or as an act of legerdemain by which miracles may be performed, regardless of the state of him who offers the prayer. While it is, as has been proved in numberless cases, one of the most powerful forces in the world, it is not a force which can be effectively handled by anybody, whatever his attitude. Hence so many millions never ask aright.

To ask aright, which is to ask and surely receive, one must come into right relations with the things asked. In other words, he must make himself a magnet for the drawing of all things which he would have. The declaration "To him that hath it shall be given" has been considered by many a "hard saying," but it is simply the statement of a scientific principle. The same truth is expressed by the proverb, "like attracts like." Having a little money, a little authority, a little skill, one is in a position to ask aright, that is, effectively, for more money, more authority, more skill, and to finally command all those things which money, authority, skill, bring. That which he has is a magnet for more.

The whole matter simply resolves itself into this truth, that according to one's becoming will be his having and holding. Someone will say, very truly and aptly, that many have authority, positions of trust, and large salaries or incomes who cannot by character, intelligence, or skill command them. Very true! But, mark you, such people never do *command*—even as they could never, by inherent right of capability demand—their positions. Again, mark the words having and *holding*. There is a having that is worse than denial, a holding that is torture. A boy who had attended a circus became wild with desire to ride, standing, a barebacked horse. His only riding had been on a slow, safe horse, and with a saddle.

But the bareback riding having for him so great a fascination, he resolved to try it at all costs. He took secretly a spirited young horse from his uncle's stable, and after many attempts succeeded, by digging his bare toes desperately into the flanks of the colt, in riding a little way with the horse in an easy trot. But he could not, of course, ride well or safely, and he was so frightened that for the rest of the day he could not eat, study, or play, and was startled at every sound. He had secured the coveted delight, and it proved worse than denial. But the next day he saw one of the circus riders out on his horse for an airing, and plucked up courage to accost him, and to offer him a half-dollar—all the money he had—if he would teach him bareback riding. The young horse was again secretly taken from the stable, and, at a safe distance, the boy mounted. The circus rider, standing easily and confidently on his own horse, met with his firm hand the boy's extended fingers, and so, holding and steadying him, the two cantered on for some distance, the boy feeling comparatively safe. After half an hour the circus rider, remarking that he "reckoned he had earned his half-dollar," rode away, leaving the boy behind. The latter, made reckless by the time spent with his late companion, determined to ride on alone, although, the feeling that he might at any moment lose his balance and be thrown, haunted him, and made his ride anything but a pleasure or a triumph. Finally he was thrown. Striking against a heap of stones, he was so cut and bruised that it was months before he could walk without pain, or be about the normal work and pleasures of a boy's life. The longed-for holding had proved a torture, and ended in disaster.

He who cannot, by the possession of capability, authority, or skill, command the things of which he has, by unwise or unjust influence, bribery, or other illegitimate means, become possessed, has little or no satisfaction in them. He may find some expert who for a compensation—many times all the unfit bidder for his services possesses—will consent to steady and coach him for a while, and so make him feel comparatively safe; but such a helper is apt to soon "reckon that he has earned his half-dollar," and to leave his late employer to plunge recklessly along in a position which experience and fitness have in nowise taught him to occupy, on a steed which is almost certain, in the end, to dislodge him, to his long pain and disaster, on the rocks of criticism, derision, distrust, and the utter demoralization of self-respect and character. Even if he keeps getting new steeds and new coaches and steadiers, he will always lack the poise and confidence which comes from the consciousness of being *master* of a subject or situation, and, consequently, that happiness which everyone expects, and should expect, as the reward of his labors. He cannot ask aright.

"But," someone says, "if gaining is a matter of already having, all one has to do is to possess himself of some money, or skill, or whatever he may wish more of, and proceed, by the magnet system, to get more and more. This needs no occult practices."

But to secure the having which will insure a happiness-making, satisfactory holding, and to become perfectly certain that you can ask aright, and therefore count always on receiving, you must *establish* your magnet. Mind the word *establish*. You must begin with just what you have, which is, in a multitude of cases, simply desire. Make that desire a *willing* to have. Then put, and *keep*, yourself in touch with those influences which can, and when invited will, give you the wisdom and the opportunity to add to your knowledge and skill, and to answer your own prayers. Prayer is sometimes answered instantly, but in these cases the ones who pray are ready for the thing for which they pray. They can ask aright. They already possess something which makes them able to command that which they desire. Many times it is an intense faith which vibrates through and dominates the whole being, and sets in motion causes which at once create the thing or condition required, as Jesus materialized the bread and turned the water into wine. This is the faith of which the Master spoke as being able to move mountains. It is the entire domination and consciousness of the All-Force which the Christ was always able to utilize.

Right here is the place to burn in upon your memory the truth that *he who would accomplish as the Christ accomplished must live as the Christ lived.*

Can another ever hope to accomplish as the Christ accomplished? His own words were, "Greater things shall ye do because I go to the Father."

One great fact must never be lost sight of. He who is to grow from strength to strength, from ability to ability, from possession to possession, and so, from living like the Christ to come more and more to create and command like the Christ, must stay where the Christ influences can reach and control him, and, through him, his affairs. "Having done all, stand," said St. Paul. All the promises of Christ are, must necessarily be, to those who *abide* in the atmosphere where such promises can be made good. One who tries to overcome and become one day or one hour, and allows bad habits, bitterness, hatred, unjust calculations or transactions to have sway the next, might as well try to grow a hardy plant by keeping it one day in rich loam and the next transplanting it to sand or frozen earth. In the soil and atmosphere of purity, of patience, of steadfastness, of growth, must be nurtured the character plant which is to yield, on demand, satisfying fruits for soul and body.

49

Another thing to remember is that the answer to prayer, or demand, is gained by causes being put in motion to bring about results, and must have time to do their work. What would you think of one who should give a tailor an order for a suit of clothes, and become discouraged and skeptical of ever receiving it because it was not ready for him in a few minutes, or a few hours? Suppose, because of this delay, he let the matter of the suit drift out of his mind, and did not apply to the tailor again? The fact is patent that he would never get the garments. Multitudes are as unreasoning and unreasonable concerning prayer, or demand, as this man would be about his suit, and by their impatience, skepticism, and failure to keep the coveted thing in mind and before the forces which can grant it, never receive it.

Finally, never be content with any receiving which does not include peace and happiness, the twin prizes which all the wealth, all the toil, all the prayers of mankind are intended to purchase.

After a time, if you are faithful in your observances of those practices which keep you in effective touch with your base of supplies, all that pertains to the world of spiritual force, peace, and happiness will become as natural to your perception and your use as are fins to the fish or wings to the bird; and you will realize that not merely in theory, but in actuality, you are "one with the Father."

SUMMARY AND EXERCISE:

If one asks aright, he cannot be denied, he must possess something if he is to command something. In order to possess something, he must be something. The nearer he grows to the Christ likeness, the more power he has to command. One is usually given the power to answer his own prayers. Spiritual strength to gain the things one desires must be fostered and grown in the God-atmosphere. The spiritual life, by being constantly lived, becomes the natural life.

Say in the silence: *I will to begin now, with just what I have, to add continually to my knowledge of* (whatever you wish) *and my skill in* (whatever you desire to do). *I will to remain in touch with the Divine Wisdom and Power which will teach and direct me, and open for me the opportunities which I need. I will to go on from knowledge to knowledge, from strength to strength, from character to character, until I feel myself one with God.*

THE MAGIC SEVEN

Proudly brought to you by
JonRose Publishing
www.JonRosePublishing.com

Other titles available from JonRose Publishing

The Science of Getting Rich
by Wallace D. Wattles

Thought Vibration
By William Walker Atkinson

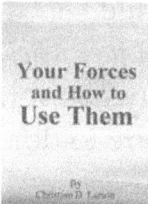

Your Forces and How to Use Them
by Christian D. Larson

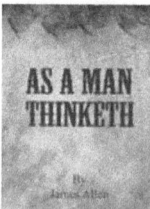

As A Man Thinketh
by James Allen

The Law of Success in Sixteen Lessons
by Napoleon Hill

Think and Grow Rich
by Napoleon Hill

www.ingramcontent.com/pod-product-compliance
Lightning Source LLC
Chambersburg PA
CBHW060610030426
42337CB00018B/3032